Gavin Jerome's

COMEDY COLLEGE
How-To-Handbook

The Definitive Guide To
Using Humor Effectively

**PUBLISHED
BY**

GOON BROS.
NOVELTY EXCELLENCE SINCE 4 O'CLOCK THIS MORNING

Gavin Jerome's
Comedy College How-To-Handbook:
The Definitive Guide to Using Humor Effectively
Copyright,© 1997 by Gavin Jerome.

Graphic design and layout by:

12308 S. CREST OLATHE, KS 66061
PHONE/FAX: (913)780-5975

Gavin Jerome's Comedy College
P.O. Box 393
Ankeny, IA 50021

Telephone orders: Gavin Jerome, Inc.:
1-800-96-GAVIN

Dedication

This book is dedicated to all the comedians past, present, and future who go about the business of making people laugh. May you never cease your efforts to save the world one laugh at a time.

Acknowledgments

To Sandra,
who never laughed at me when I said I wanted to become a comedian.

To Tom,
I would not be where I am without your help. Everything I know about this business, I learned from you. Your patience, guidance and wisdom have been much appreciated. You are a class act, a consummate professional and a true friend.

To Lisa,
Without your help in the beginning, none of this would have been possible.

<u>Page</u>

Exercise

PROLOGUE
Nobody Read The Memo

I thought I was funny. I'd gotten laughs at several open-mic comedy nights in my home town. I was a huge hit at the college talent show. I even placed second at an amateur comedy competition. (Second prize was a dinner for two; I found out afterward that "dinner" did not include appetizers or desserts. Winning second prize ended up costing me $14.97.)

While working at a local comedy club, I met a touring comedian. He got me a paid road gig as his opening act. By the time they deducted my meals and all the drinks I bought for myself and my friends, I ended up clearing $18.00. I was ecstatic. I had only been in the comedy business three months and already I was making the big money.

No doubt about it, I was going to be the next comedy superstar. I packed up my jokes and a few clothes and headed to L.A. It wouldn't take long for them to discover such an obvious talent. I had my pen in hand as I disembarked from the plane, ready to sign that movie or T.V. deal. I only hoped that I would be able to choose the one that was "right" for me from all of the offers that I was about to receive. I looked around the terminal. No paparazzi. No casting directors, agents, or talent scouts. Apparently, nobody had read the memo.

I was fortunate enough to land a job at one of L.A.'s premier showcase comedy clubs. Several now famous comedians had already been discovered there. My first night was a Tuesday, pro-celebrity work-out night. Big name after big name got up and worked on new material. Awestruck, I could only look at my own comedy notebook. The one filled with the anecdotes, gags, and one-liners that were going to take me to the top. I flipped gingerly through the pages, comparing my work to the work I had just witnessed. Disgusted, I threw my notebook into the trash. I knew absolutely nothing about stand-up comedy. It was then that I realized I had a long, long road ahead.

INTRODUCTION

The esteemed author E.B. White once wrote, "Dissecting humor is like dissecting a frog, both die in the process." I have always thought that quote was hogwash. But every book on comedy I have ever read has included this quote. Just to prove to all the scholars and critics that I have done my research, I have included it as well. Comedy doesn't need to die when dissected. It all depends on the skill of the surgeon holding the scalpel.

Comedy is a skill, like welding, carpentry, or plumbing. Through careful study and practice over a number of years, almost anyone can reach the level of master craftsman. As in any science, there are certain fundamentals, formulas, and rules. Comedy, however, is not an exact science. Humor is subjective. One person may find a particular joke hysterical; another will groan at it. Any book that pretends to be the "be all, end all" tome on comedy is really misleading its reader. Still, if someone were truly interested in learning this craft, careful study of the masters reveals a multitude of common techniques that every great comedian employs. This book is a study of these ideas and techniques. Keep in mind, however, **there is no quick fix**. The subtle skills and techniques may take years to master. Like any other skill, comedy must be practiced and honed at every opportunity. Granted, there are a few comedians who have achieved success while flying in the face of every comedy convention. But for the beginner, this book should go a long way in shedding light on the mysterious science called comedy.

CHAPTER ONE
Humor Basics

What is comedy? Ask one hundred people that question and you will get one hundred different answers. I suppose you could look up the word in the dictionary. A word of caution though. Merriam Webster never had to close the midnight comedy show on St. Patrick's Day in Kansas City. Merriam Webster never had to follow several boring speeches before giving the keynote address at the Women's Auxiliary Luncheon. Many famous comedians have tried to define comedy as well. Steve Allen once defined comedy as "tragedy plus time." That's a little too deep for me. One of my favorite comedians, Steve Martin, defined comedy as "the ability to make someone laugh without making them puke." Although this is a decent definition, it is a little messy. My brother Steve defines comedy as a wedgie where my underwear is pulled up high enough to clear my shoulder blades. Again, not a bad definition, but none the less, a painful one. It seems that everyone named Steve has a definition of comedy. So for our purposes, we need a working definition of comedy.[1]

Comedy is:
Making a connection with the audience
that produces laughter.

---

[1] Throughout this book the terms **comedy** and **humor** will be used interchangeably. Comedian will refer to anyone using humor or comedy in public speaking. For the sake of brevity the pronoun "he" will be used with the full understanding that it applies to any budding Letterman or Whoopi who reads my text.

This is a three part sentence. In order to be an effective comedian, all three parts of this definition must be understood. To make it easier, I will break it down.

1. Making a connection: If the audience doesn't connect with you, they won't laugh. The first step in creating comedy is bridging the gap between performer and audience member. You must capture the audience's attention. The two ways to connect with them are stage presence and material; what you say and how you say it. George Carlin is one of the most brilliant comedians of our time. Many people are unable to get past his "blue" language so they don't enjoy his humor. Similarly, Andrew Dice Clay achieved remarkable success as a stand-up comedian. His persona, however, offended and angered many. He couldn't connect with much of his audience and his career was short-lived. Making a connection is the most important thing for a comedian to do.

2. With the audience: This is a no-brainer, but it must be mentioned. You can stand in front of a mirror in your basement and tell joke after joke, but you are not creating comedy. The knock you are about to hear isn't opportunity, but men with butterfly nets coming to take you away. The size of the audience doesn't matter. In order to create comedy you must perform for someone else besides yourself.

3. That produces laughter: This is a measuring stick. If your connection with the audience does not produce laughter, then you are a science teacher, a politician(1) a psychic friend working the hotline. You must get laughs. If you don't, then you are not a comedian.

If laughter is the holy grail which all comedians pursue, then we must define laughter as well.

---

(1) Authors note. Given that most politicians are in fact ridiculous comedians, it is the author's hope not to confuse the reader with this analogy.

Laughter is:
An emotional release of
humorous tension.

More important than a clinical definition of humor are reasons why we laugh. I have identified three main reasons why people laugh.

1. Surprise
2. Superiority
3. Release

1. Surprise is the most important element of comedy. People laugh if the comedy material takes them in an unexpected direction. It is the comedian's job to pull the rug out from under the listener at every opportunity. Comedy is not like music. If you hear the same joke again and again, it loses some of its entertainment value .

2. Superiority. A common technique used by comedians is to place themselves or another in a foolish position. The audience laughs because they are glad it's not them. It becomes even funnier if the target of the joke is in a position of power greater than the listener. The audience will laugh because they feel superior.

3. Release. Sometimes tension builds up and laughter ensues to release that tension. We've all heard the phrase, "nervous laughter". When we do something clumsy or foolish, many times we laugh it off to relieve the embarrassment.

Tension can also occur as the result of a disturbance while you are performing. Tension can sometimes happen when the performer makes a mistake or forgets a joke. A humorous quip can help the audience release that tension.

Let me take a moment and address a common misconception that I encounter all the time. Many people think that creating humor is a mystical process of divine inspiration bestowed by the comedy gods upon a chosen few. Nothing could be further from the truth. You must look at comedy or humor as a muscle. The more you use it, the stronger it will become. To illustrate this point, I will use two examples. Arnold Schwartzenegger is one of Hollywood's biggest stars. He makes 20 million dollars per picture and I can't understand a single word he says. But let's face it, nobody goes to see his movies for the great dialogue. You will never hear Arnold's name mentioned after the phrase, "the Oscar goes to..." But that is not what he is selling. People go to his movies to see those incredible muscles. Do you think he looked that way the first time he walked into a gym? No. Unfortunately for Arnold, he probably looked a little bit like me. But the difference is that he worked at it. Day after day, week after week, year after year until he developed the physique he currently displays.

Jerry Seinfeld is, in my opinion, the 90's greatest comedian. I saw an interview recently where he was asked what it was like when he was just starting out. His response was one I will never forget. He said, "When I was starting out, I used to rush my jokes just to get to the funny one." To me, that says it all. The 90's greatest comedian admitted on national television that he stank when he started out. But he worked on it. Day after day, week after week, year after year until he built his humor muscle to the point where it is today. The same is true of today's successful comedians. They didn't start out funny. They worked at it night after night, playing comedy clubs, colleges, and conventions. The good ones make it appear effortless. What we don't see are the years spent training their humor muscle in dive bars for five drunks at two o'clock in the morning. You too, must begin to develop your humor muscle. I have identified the four basic parts of your humor muscle. They are:

1. Sense of humor
2. Joke writing
3. Joke delivery
4. Tricks of the trade

The next few chapters will break down each of these important skills.

Go
Jest
Young man!

CHAPTER TWO
Sense of Humor

In school we learned that everyone has 5 senses: Sight, smell, touch, taste, and sound. I believe there are 6. To that list you must add a sense of humor. Everyone has a sense of humor. Many may argue this point. We have all said it from time to time. "So and so just doesn't have a sense of humor." Everyone has a sense of humor, some are just more developed than others. I have never met anyone who did not want to improve their sense of humor. But like everything else in life, it must be worked at. In order to improve your sense of humor we must first define what it is.

Sense of humor is:
The ability to look at things from a whimsical or offbeat perspective.

A person with a good sense of humor generally is able to perceive relationships that others miss. They also exhibit a great deal of creativity in their thinking. People with a good sense of humor generally look at the glass as being half full as opposed to half empty. Having a good sense of humor makes it a little easier to cope with life's trials and tribulations.

To improve your sense of humor you must focus on the **Three L's.**

LOOK

LISTEN

LOG

LOOK

A person with a good sense of humor actively searches for the humor in every situation. A multitude of funny things happen around you everyday. The problem is that most people are too bogged down with life to notice. Someone with a good sense of humor always keeps his eyes open.

You must **Look** at:
Things as they happen.
Things as they could have happened.
The incongruities of what happened.

LISTEN

Listening is the simplest way to develop a sense of humor. It has been said that no human endeavor is so easily faked and so difficult to do well. At first not everyone may be able to write or tell a joke, but everyone can listen to one. Keep in mind that hearing and listening are two different things. We all have had our hearing checked. When was the last time we had our listening checked?

You must **Listen** to:
What people say.
What people don't say.
Your inner voice.

LOG

You never know when something funny will pop into your head. But as fast as an idea pops into your head , it will pop back out. If you write it down, it will be yours forever. If you don't, it may be gone for good. Keep a notebook of jokes, thoughts, or ideas. Carry it with you at all times. Many people keep a joke file, similar to a recipe file, with their jokes, thoughts or ideas on index cards. Always log your funny ideas so you can refer to them later.

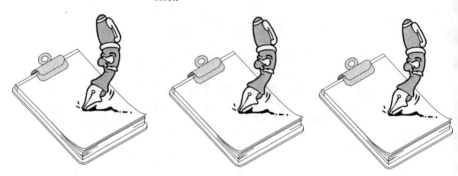

If you are reading this book, you must have at least a little sense of humor. You may be one of the few people in this world who had their sense of humor surgically removed. If that is the case, you need a humor transplant, which is beyond the scope of this book. Even if you consider yourself humor impaired, at least you have shown the desire to improve your ability to use and enjoy humor. As long as you have the desire, there is hope.

I hear it all the time. "My friends think I'm funny." Or, "everybody says I should be a comedian". Terrific. I am sure you are a riot. But you must understand there are three kinds of funny.

1. Family room funny
2. Water cooler funny
3. Spotlight funny

Three Kinds of Funny

Family room funny

Someone who is family room funny is a crack-up for both family and friends. This type of person is fun, zany, and usually a joy to be around. It is easiest to be family room funny because the people you are joking with and for are those who hopefully already know and like you. This type of humor relies on "off the cuff" remarks or quips that the humorist fires back at the listeners.

Water cooler funny

People who are water cooler funny have the ability to be cut-ups at work. Joking with co-workers can liven up a mundane and boring work space. It is easy to be water cooler funny. Co-workers and colleagues are so starved for humor that even the smallest amount of wit can produce gales of laughter.

Spotlight funny

Now this is the tough one. Having the ability to be funny on demand is difficult indeed.
If you are spotlight funny, you can make an audience laugh that has paid their hard earned money to be entertained. The pressures of a spotlight funny person are much greater. The audience expects you to be funny. There is little margin for error. Much of the audience are strangers who could care less about you personally. Whether you want to be spotlight funny or just find more humor in your family room or near your water cooler, the following tips, tricks and techniques will help you.

Don't forget "Smells Funny!"

> Your mouth is your greatest weapon... don't shoot it off son.

Arm Yourself

The first exercise you must complete is to arm yourself with the weapons of a comedian. A comedian's most effective weapons are his mouth and mind. The second is the pen and paper which they use to write their jokes. Go out and purchase the following items:

1. One spiral notebook or legal pad used only for comedy.

2. One small memo notebook.

3. Writing utensils (pens or pencils, whatever you prefer).

As a budding humorist you will go through a ton of paper. Make sure you are never without your little memo pad. So many great jokes and ideas have been lost because there were no pens or notebooks nearby. Never let that happen to you.

Exercise One
Laugh At Yourself

The first step in improving your sense of humor is improving your ability to laugh at yourself. Too many of us in this world take ourselves too seriously. Lighten up a little. People are funny. Today you will do and say many funny, silly, or stupid things. Begin by keeping track of these things. Take a second to write down what you did or said that was even a little bit humorous. Remember it only has to be funny to you. Do this for a week and you will improve your ability to laugh at yourself. (If you are one of those people who doesn't like to mess up their shiny new book, this exercise and the ones to follow can be done on a separate sheet of paper.)

1.
2.
3.
4.
5.
6.
7.
8.
9.
10.
11.
12.
13.
14.
15.

Exercise Two
<u>Laugh with Others</u>

Unless you are in solitary at Riker's Island prison, your world is filled with interesting people. They also will do and say many funny things during the course of a day. If you are paying attention, you may be able to pick up something fun. A word of caution, the title of this exercise is laugh with others. This is not an accident. As a rule, you laugh at yourself and **with** others. As you work on this exercise, please don't be one of those annoying people who follows others around with a notebook waiting for something to happen. Not only will nothing funny occur, but you will irritate the people around you. Pay attention and jot things down when you are alone.

<u>Laugh with Others List</u>

1.	
2.	
3.	
4.	
5.	
6.	
7.	
8.	
9.	
10.	
11.	
12.	
13.	
14.	
15.	

CHAPTER THREE
Frame of Mind

In my opinion the most important skill a budding new comedian can possess is the ability to write clever, original material. This skill is the focus of the majority of this book. Like your comedy muscle, writing jokes is a skill that develops the more it is used.

The first important step to joke writing is being in the proper frame of mind. This always reminds me of an old Steve Martin routine. Steve is asked "How can you be so funny?" He replies, "Before I go on stage I put a slice of bologna in each of my shoes. When I'm on stage, I **feel** funny."

I don't advocate that anyone actually do this. First of all, the money spent on cold cuts over the course of your comedy career will drive you to the poor house. Secondly, the combination of rancid meat and sweaty foot odor could be lethal.

The principle behind this idea is solid. To be your funniest, you have to put your mind in a funny mood. This can be accomplished many ways. This exercise has helped many of my students.

Exercise Three
Funny Thought List

Take a moment and let your mind wander to things that you think are funny. It can be anything, (a funny joke you heard on television, a funny face your roommate made, a favorite cartoon). Anything that makes you laugh you should write down on paper. Use the back of this page or a separate sheet of paper if you need extra space.

"The Funny Thought List"

1.

2.

3.

4.

5.

6.

7.

8.

9.

10.

Got your list made? Good. Now keep this handy every time you sit down to write jokes. Before putting pen to paper, take out this list and review it. It will make you chuckle and put you in the proper frame of mind to write jokes.

In a perfect world, our minds would be free to write jokes all the time. But let's face it, if we lived in a perfect world, disco would never have made a come back. Pressures at work and in your personal life can clutter up your mind, forming a barrier to creativity. You must learn to put these problems aside for a little while so you can write comedy. There is an exercise called "bracketing" that helps clear a writer's mind so that the writing process is easier.

Exercise Four
Bracketing

Take a piece of paper and write down all of the things that are bothering you. Write down all of things that are preventing you from focusing on comedy. Try to find at least five.

Take a moment and look at your list. Cool, huh? Now take that piece of paper and crumple it up into a little ball. Throw it into the trash, against the wall, or slam it down on the floor. Feels good, doesn't it? You have both literally and figuratively cleared your mind for the task ahead.

CHAPTER FOUR
Source of Comedy

A common question I hear from people starting out is, "How do you come up with your comedy ideas?" Another common comment is, "I can't think of anything funny. Where do I start?"

Here are my three favorite sources of comedy:

Personal Experiences
Print Media
Broadcast Media

Personal experiences. Personal experiences are the most important source of comedy. Each of us bring our own different life experiences to the comedy table. We all have unique qualities that no one else possesses. You must look inward and begin to laugh at yourself before you can laugh at others. No other source of comedy has such rich potential for original material.

Print media. Print media is defined as anything on a printed page. This includes newspapers, books, or magazines. The plain fact is that truth is funnier than fiction. Everyday, numerous news items are printed in the daily papers. Read the paper and anything else you can get your hands on. To the trained eye, comedy literally jumps off the pages into a comedian's lap. If you are not paying attention to current events you are missing a huge opportunity for finding comedy.

Broadcast media. Broadcast media is defined as anything that can be viewed or that is presented to the viewer. This includes television, radio, and movies. The wonderful thing about broadcast media is that the majority of the audience will have similar exposure to it. It's a great source of comedy, so don't overlook it.

Other Sources. It is important to note that there may be other sources of comedy that fall in between the definitions presented above. The internet is an example of a new kind of media that has a growing audience. Just keep in mind that not everyone has access to it. Be sure to assess your audience before using cyber-space as a Source of material.

You will probably be able to think of many other sources of comedy once you start to flex your humor muscle. These will give you a good place to start.

Exercise Five

Newspaper Items

Truth is funnier than fiction. Take a copy of any newspaper. (I prefer USA Today. It has such pretty colors). Read over the newspaper for any news item or headline that strikes you as funny.

NEWSPAPER ITEMS:

1.
2.
3.
4.
5.
6.
7.
8.
9.
10.
11.
12.
13.
14.
15.

Exercise Six
Broadcast Media

In the 90's, almost everyone has a T.V. When doing an exercise for broadcast media, the idiot box is a great place to start. Watch a little television. Write down a list of ideas you got from watching T.V. If you get stuck, focus on the commercials, they are the easiest.

T.V. Ideas

1.	
2.	
3.	
4.	
5.	
6.	
7.	
8.	
9.	
10.	
11.	
12.	
13.	
14.	
15.	

CHAPTER FIVE
IBET

Joke writing consists of a simple four step process. I know what you are saying, "Yeah, I bet it does!" You would be exactly right.

The four steps to joke writing are:

Idea

Brainstorming

Editing

Tie together

This acronym will help you remember what to do next if you get stuck. Not everybody writes like this. Sometimes a finished joke will just pop into your head. More often than not, you will have to work at it. If you follow these steps, joke writing will be much easier.

 ## The Faucet Principle

When it comes to joke writing, not everyone creates the same way. Some people can sit down at a typewriter and make the jokes flow. Others, like myself, have to wait for that spurt of creativity. I call this phenomenon in comedy writing "the faucet". Sometimes your creative faucet is on and the ideas are gushing out. Other times it is bone dry and no amount of forcing the knobs will get it going. When this occurs it is best not to force it.

Careful examination will show that a pattern emerges. Certain circumstances and situations are more conducive to an open faucet. A smart comic is one who identifies these circumstances and cultivates them. For example, I am the most creative in the car and in the shower. (Freud would have a field day with that one!) When I am trying to come up with new material I take both long drives and long showers . (If I could figure out how to shower while driving I'd be set.)

A word to the wise, when the faucet is open and running, forsake everything else and catch every last drop of your creativity. You never know when it will be gushing again. The stronger your humor muscle, the more often the faucet will be open and running.

There is one thing you can do to make joke writing easier. It is so important I have labeled it The "Secret" To Joke Writing. It is so valuable it is worth the price of this book. Are you ready?

Exercise Seven
The Secret to Joke Writing

A line down the middle of the page? You have got to be kidding! That's the secret of joke writing? Believe it or not, this tool used correctly will help you to better write and organize your jokes.

Let me show you what I mean. We first need to start with an idea for a joke. The best opening a comedian can use is a quick joke about themselves. Since one of the first things people notice about me is my hair, we will use my hair as our first joke idea.

Once I have my subject, I draw a line down the middle of the page. On the left hand side I write the premise, or joke idea. In this case, it is **Gavin's Hair.**

Gavin's Hair

(complete with own zip code)

Gavin

(High School Photo)

PREMISE	
Gavin's Hair	

Terrific! We are a fourth of the way home!

The next stage in the **IBET** process is **B** for **Brainstorming.** I take a moment to brainstorm everything I can about my hair. I record my ideas on the right hand side of the page. Ask questions during the brainstorming stage or let your mind be creative.

My finished product looks like this:

PREMISE	IDEAS
Gavin's Hair 	LOOKS LIKE ELVIS EYE CATCHING WIND TUNNEL ROGAINE RECEDING HAIRLINE LIGHT SOCKET MUCH TALLER THINGS LIVING IN MY HAIR CHIA PET NOT REAL HAIR CARE PRODUCTS GIRLFRIEND PROBLEMS HAIR DRESSER TOUCAN SAM HAIR CLUB FOR MEN COWLICK BIG HAIR MALL BANGS PATTI LABELLE DON KING BLOW DRYER CONVERTIBLE DIPPITY DOO FRIGHTENED

Great! I am now half way home!

   With brainstorming done, I move on to the next phase of **IBET** -- **E** for **Edit**. Looking over the right side of my page, I circle the best ideas. These are the unique or interesting ideas that may lend themselves to comedy. To make things easier, I get out a fresh sheet of paper. (You may go through a lot of paper. Stock up!) I again draw a line down the middle of the page. I transfer these ideas to the left side of page two. I find it easier to separate my good ideas. Half the battle of writing jokes is good organization.

My finished product looks like this:

PREMISE	IDEAS
Gavin's Hair 	**LOOKS LIKE ELVIS** **BIG HAIR** **GIRLFRIEND PROBLEMS** **BLOW DRYER** **THINGS LIVING IN MY HAIR**

Fabulous! We are heading down the home stretch!

In the final stage, I write the actual jokes. The final stage of the **IBET** process is **T**, for **Tie Together**. Here are the jokes I developed from the selected ideas.

JOKES

I know what you're thinking ... Elvis died and left me his hair.

I am about 9.6 on the big hair meter.

My girlfriend is using me. Not for sex, but for my hair care secrets.

My blow-dryer has three speeds: high, low, and fission.

Yesterday I ran my fingers through my hair...I found Jimmy Hoffa.

Not bad for five minutes worth of work. I realize that I went through the four steps very quickly. Fear not. The next few chapters will break down each step, making the whole process clearer.

CHAPTER SIX
Ideas

Every joke must start somewhere. It starts with an idea or premise. Simply put, **the idea or premise is the subject of your joke.** The number of premises for jokes are limited only by your imagination. A joke idea can be very specific or very broad. The more original the premise, the better your joke will be.

The easiest way to begin is to start with a statement of fact. This can be anything:

> I am really gaining weight...
> My neighbor is stupid...
> My spouse and I had a fight.
> The Chicago Cubs lost again...
> Fast food restaurants never get my order right,,,

Truth is one of the most important elements in humor. A good comedian takes a common truth or fact and distorts it or comments on it in such a way as to really strike a chord with the audience members.

A joke idea can be very specific or very broad. The thing to remember is to make it as original as possible. Avoid common premises and ideas. As you watch other comedians you will notice many of the same premises begin to emerge. Steer clear of them if you can. The more original the premise, the better your joke will be.

It is best to start with a statement that generally interests you. It works better to write about something you know. Don't try to write a routine on fast food if you never eat out. If you want to write fat jokes but are skinny as a rail, leave them to somebody else.

The next exercise will help to get you started.

Exercise Eight
Personal Trait Exercise

Take a minute and write down everything you can think of that is uniquely you. It can be anything. What you look like, your job, interesting hobbies or values. It can be anything that describes you as a person.

1.	
2.	
3.	
4.	
5.	
6.	
7.	
8.	
9.	
10.	
11.	
12.	
13.	
14.	
15.	

CHAPTER SEVEN
Brainstorming

We've all heard the term "brainstorming".

Brainstorming is: The creative process for generating a large number of ideas.

Sounds simple, right? Wrong! Brainstorming is an important skill to master. You must follow certain rules in order to brainstorm effectively.

Rule 1. Quantity. The object is to come up with as many ideas as possible. Don't worry about quality. This leads to rule 2.

Rule 2. No put downs or evaluations. Do not try to judge each of the ideas. This comes later. If you stop to consider the merit of any thought, it de-rails the process. Write down each idea no matter how silly, which is rule 3.

Rule 3. Record each idea. You must write down everything. In a good brainstorming session you should be writing furiously. If an idea is not recorded it may be lost when you try to think of it again. Also, writing down each idea may lead you in another direction.

Rule 4. Piggyback; expand on a previous idea. A thought may lead you in a different direction. That is great. Go with it. Good brainstorming involves letting yourself explore all possible avenues.

Rule 5. Encourage zany, far-out ideas. This is the time to get wild. Nothing is too far-fetched. Some of the best comedy ideas arise when you "step outside the box". Don't be afraid to get really creative. Usually the far-out ideas happen when the obvious ones have been exhausted.

Rule 6. Set a time limit. In brainstorming, like anything else, there is a point of diminishing returns. If you set a time limit, it forces you to stay focused and creates a sense of urgency. There is no set time limit to use. Generally speaking, the best ideas are developed in the first 10 minutes of brainstorming. If the ideas are flowing, by all means keep going.

The most common mistake made in brainstorming is looking at things from only one angle. I like to look at brainstorming like spokes coming out of a wheel.

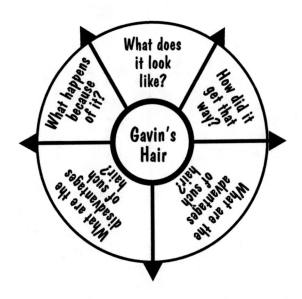

Keep turning the wheel and asking different questions. By doing that, your brainstorms will be less one dimensional.

Exercise Nine
Brainstorming Your Idea

Pick an idea, or premise from one of the exercises that you completed in the last chapter. On the left hand side of the following page, write the premise down. Now, using the brainstorming skills that you just learned, write down as many ideas about your premise as you can come up with. Try to fill all the spaces provided.

Brainstorming

PREMISE	IDEAS

Exercise Nine
Brainstorming Your Idea

Remember those print media ideas you generated in exercise 5 (page 19)? Pick your favorite one and then brainstorm it!

PRINT MEDIA PREMISE	BRAINSTORM

Exercise Eleven
Broadcast Media

Remember those broadcast media ideas you generated in exercise 6 (page 20)? Pick your favorite one and then brainstorm it!

Broadcast Media Premise	Brainstorm

Exercise Twelve
Personal Trait Exercise

Remember those personal trait ideas you generated in exercise 8 (page 27)?
Pick your favorite one and then brainstorm it!

Personal Trait	Brainstorm

CHAPTER EIGHT
Editing

One of the toughest hurdles you face as a new comedian is that inner critic that evaluates everything you write. We've all heard that inner voice:

> "You're not funny...."
> "That joke stinks...."
> "Don't quit your day job...."

The inner critic is not a bad thing. It is the inner critic that keeps you from falling on your face. The mistake that many people make is letting this critic into the joke writing process too early. It is only in the third step (editing) that we listen to our internal Siskel and Ebert.

It is now on this stage where the joke begins to take shape. During the brainstorming stage I warned you not to evaluate your ideas. The editing stage is where you separate the wheat from the chaff.

Look at the right side of the exercise you just completed. You now have the job of sifting for the gold nuggets. Search for things that may be funny. In many cases, you may need to edit the good ideas even further. I suggest doing this by asking questions.

Rudyard Kipling once said, "I have 6 friends that taught me all I know,

WHO WHAT WHEN WHERE WHY HOW

To these six I will add two others...I will add

WHEXT and WHIF

These are short for **"What Next"** and **"What If"**. By asking questions of your ideas, you flesh them out even further.

Turn back to my hair example in chapter five. Some questions I might ask to flesh out some of the humor from my brainstorms are:

Why does my hair look like Elvis?
How does my hair cause girlfriend problems?
What could be living in my hair?
What if I had a special hair dyer?
Where did I get my haircut?

Gavin's
Inner Voice

Often I am asked, "How do I know if any idea is funny?" My answer is a simple one. Listen to your inner critic. Does the idea make you laugh? Can you see potential for a joke there? The more you develop your humor muscle, the better your internal critic will become. In the early stages you may want to seek out other opinions. A word of caution- most people will resist humor if they think you are trying to be funny. The best way to test a joke is to slip it into normal conversation.

Please...
No more
jokes!

Getting help from friends and family can be tricky as well. A spouse or parent may tell you something is funny just to spare your feelings. My wife has been my sounding board for years. She has had the exact same response to every joke I have ever told her. She never laughs. She just smiles and says "That's good, Dear." I listen to myself and how the joke sounds to me when I tell it. If I like it, then I'll keep it. In short, trust your instincts .

The other thing that can be helpful is a writing partner. In comedy writing, two or more heads are better than one. Find someone with a similar interest in comedy. Other people may perceive relationships and inconsistencies that you miss. Writing with a partner can add another dimension to your material.

CHAPTER NINE
WORDACE

Okay, here we are, the moment of truth. We must take our edited ideas and turn them into a joke. That may seem like a difficult task. The most critical part of the joke is the punch line. The most common mistake a beginning joke writer makes is not finishing a good idea with a solid punch line. To make this task easier, I have identified seven basic formulas a punch line can take. Using these formulas will help add punch to your punch lines.

To help you remember the formulas, I created **WORDACE** (I know this borders on "acronym abuse.")

WORDACE is as follows:

Word Play

Observation

Reverse

Definition

Analogy

Combination

Exaggeration

Word play is a broad category that often gets laughs from misuse or uncommon use of words or cliches. There are many different types of word play. I will mention a few.

Commonly regarded as the lowest form of humor, puns are humorous misuses of words that sound alike but have different meanings.

For example:

> **How do trains hear?**
> **Through their engineers.**
>
> **What does a grape say when you step on it?**
> **Nothing, it just gives a little whine.**

Double entendre is a French word defined as "two meanings". A key word can be taken two different ways. The humor is usually derived from one of the meanings being off color.

For example:
> **Lawyers do it in their briefs.**
> **Doctors do it with patience.**
> **Bankers do it with interest.**

Literal Truth

Literal truth takes the literal meaning of a key word, thereby surprising the audience .

For example:

> I feel like a pizza. That's funny, you don't look like a pizza!
> (Crusty Old Joke)

My wife went window shopping, yesterday. She came home with seven windows.
(Rodney Dangerfield)

I spilled spot remover on my dog. And now he's gone.
(Steven Wright)

Cliches

Changing familiar phrases or cliches is another example of wordplay. There are two types of cliche wordplay, a reform and a take off.

Reforming a Cliche: Altering the words of a cliche.

For example:

> I will not cut off my nose to spite my race.
> (Golda Meir)

I know a transsexual who only wants to eat, drink, and be Mary.
(George Carlin)

Take Off: When you state a cliche and then go in a different direction.

For example:

> Comedy is in my blood...too bad it's not in my act.
> (Rodney Dangerfield)

I wouldn't hurt a fly...unless it was open.
(Mae West)

Oxymorons

A oxymoron is a contradiction in terms.
For example:

> Jumbo shrimp.

> Military intelligence.

> Friendly criticism.

Comedy College examples:

"I come from a "big-ass" family. There are not that
many of us...we all have big asses!"

Scott Kiefer

"I've got the here-after disease. That's when you wander
around from room to room trying to figure out what you
are here after."

Gayl Waugh

"I went to a mind reader the other day. She was big.
She was fat. She was one large medium."

Tom Bowen

"I got fired from working in a manhole because all of
my friends kept dropping in."

Steven Beets

"Ya know what really grinds my gears? Stick shifts.
Urinals really piss me off! And rodeos really chap
my ass."

Amber Darby

Exercise Thirteen
WORDPLAY

This space has been provided for you to work on writing a wordplay with one of your joke ideas, or premises from the previous chapters.

1.
2.
3.
4.
5.
6.
7.
8.
9.
10.
11.
12.
13.
14.
15.
16.
17.
18.
19.
20.

Observation

An observation draws relationships that we wouldn't normally see based on a premise that we perceive to be true. An observation points out life's incongruities. We laugh because we can relate to it. The comedian tries to make sense out of a nonsensical world.

Observations can be short one-liners, but it is preferable to use the observation as the setup and your reaction to the observation as the punch line.

Observations are fragments of data that flow through your thoughts while you are involved in everyday living.

For example:

> **Why do we park on driveways and drive on parkways?**
> (Steven Wright)

Comedy College Examples:

> **"Dating is harder when you're older. It's hard because I'm not selling the same product that I was when I was younger. That's not true, I'm still selling the same product, it's just that the merchandise has moved to a lower shelf."**
> Karen Swanson

> **"Have you ever noticed that the size of a man's belt buckle is inversely proportionate to the size of his I.Q.?"**
> Monica Lee Parker

> **"Do you get stewed tomatoes by watering your garden with beer?"**
> Tom Bowen

> **"If my clone kills your clone would it be a copy cat killing?"**
> Elaine Rockwell

Exercise Fourteen
Observation

This space has been provided for you to work on writing an observation about one of your joke ideas, or premises from the previous chapters.

1.	
2.	
3.	
4.	
5.	
6.	
7.	
8.	
9.	
10.	
11.	
12.	
13.	
14.	
15.	
16.	
17.	
18.	
19.	
20.	

Reverse

A reverse is an unexpected switch in the audience point of view in which you turn around a normal sequence of events.

A good reverse takes the listener down the garden path and then quickly changes direction.

For example:
My wife ran off with my best friend...I'm really going to miss him.
(Crusty Old Joke)

I was such an ugly kid...my mother got morning sickness after I was born.
(Rodney Dangerfield)

Comedy College Examples:

"He's a great cat. I love him. Especially when he taps on the window wanting to be let out. I'm getting kind of tired opening up that microwave. Just kidding. I would never do that to my microwave."

Tom Scorzelli

"My family was so poor, I had to wear hand-me downs. Too bad I had two older sisters."

Tom Bowen

"I've never done drugs - partially because of the danger...of having fun."

Darin Larsen

"I would never say that my mother talks too much. I wouldn't want to interrupt her."

Jay Thompson

Exercise Fifteen
Reverse

This space has been provided for you to work on writing a reverse about one of your joke ideas, or premises from the previous chapters.

1.	
2.	
3.	
4.	
5.	
6.	
7.	
8.	
9.	
10.	
11.	
12.	
13.	
14.	
15.	
16.	
17.	
18.	
19.	
20.	

Definitions

A definition joke simply defines a word in a comical way. It is similar to an exaggeration in that it magnifies an aspect of the subject to make it funny.

For example:

"Virus" is a Latin word for "Your guess is as good as mine."
(Bob Hope)

"IOWA" stands for "Idiots Out Walking About".
(Crusty Old Joke)

Comedy College Examples:

"You know what NASCAR stands for? National Association of Shirtless, Cigarette-smoking, Alcohol-guzzling Rednecks."
James, Mike & John

"Grad School is day care for people who don't want to work."
Monica Lee Parker

"When you see his truck at the grocery store, and you only shoot out one of the tires-that's my idea of reconciliation."
Jan Hicks

"How about a round of applause for the "Doctor of Comedy" - Gavin Jerome! In his case, the Phd stands for "permanent hair disorder."
Scott Kiefer

"I was at an outdoor concert. It started raining so everybody put on those garbage bags where you poke a hole for your arms and head. I thought,"Boy, this gives a whole new meaning to the phrase 'white trash'."

Jay Thompson

Exercise Sixteen
Definitions

This space has been provided for you to work on writing a definition about one of your joke ideas, or premises from the previous chapters.

1.
2.
3.
4.
5.
6.
7.
8.
9.
10.
11.
12.
13.
14.
15.
16.
17.
18.
19.
20.

Analogy

An analogy is a comparison between two things that appear dissimilar.

Here is a wonderful formula for comparing things in a humorous way. It often takes the form of:

"Im as_____ as a_____"

or

"I feel like_____"

For Example:

I was as nervous as Dan Quayle at a spelling bee.
(Crusty Old Joke)

Comedy College Examples:

I'm as nervous as Nancy Kerrigan at a pipe and steamfitters' convention.
Dennis Gibson

Reverend Phelp's chances of getting into heaven are as likely as Alanis Morrisette touring in "Up With People."
Fran Bailey

"I'm as single as a female praying mantis after sex."
Jenny Nordstrom

"I grew up in a family of 8 kids. My mom had 4 kids. My step-dad had 4 kids. Four boys. Four girls. We were like the Brady Bunch on fertility drugs."
Amy Soliday

"I started tanning. After my first session I was so red I looked like a thermometer with a beer gut."
Scott Kiefer

Exercise Seventeen
Analogy

This space has been provided for you to work on writing an analogy about one of your joke ideas, or premises from the previous chapters.

1.
2.
3.
4.
5.
6.
7.
8.
9.
10.
11.
12.
13.
14.
15.
16.
17.
18.
19.
20.

Combinations

A combination takes the characteristics from two different items and blends them together in a funny way.

Combination jokes are usually generated by listing characteristics associated with each subject. The writer then connects a characteristic from one list to a characteristic from the other list
For example:

I went out to eat at a Chinese/German restaurant. An hour after I ate I was hungry for power.

(Crusty old joke)

Comedy College Examples:

"I'm half Jewish and half Catholic. I'll force you to eat but I'll feel guilty about it afterwards."

Pam Brudno

"They're coming out with a new product. They're adding "ginkoba" to marijuana. This way, you won't be able to smoke yourself stupid."

Brandon Aschan

"I'm a single mom. I'm both the man and the woman of the house. Every morning I have to scratch myself before putting my make-up on."

Kris Keller

"I'm really proud of a process that I invented. It's called 'one step cleaning.' Now I can shampoo my cat and clean my toilet in one easy swish."

Sheri Michaels

Exercise Eighteen
Combinations

This space has been provided for you to work on writing a combination about one of your joke ideas, or premises from the previous chapters.

1.	
2.	
3.	
4.	
5.	
6.	
7.	
8.	
9.	
10.	
11.	
12.	
13.	
14.	
15.	
16.	
17.	
18.	
19.	
20.	

Exaggeration

An exaggeration joke is one in which a quality of something is stretched to the point of absurdity.

Keep in mind that an exaggeration can be stretched too far. A certain amount of realism must be maintained in order to be funny

For Example:

He was so fat, he had more chins than a Chinese phone book.
(Crusty Old Joke)

Comedy College Examples:

"I'm such a clothes horse. I don't have a closet, I have a paddock."
Jacque Johanson

"I'm getting to the age where my crows feet are sporting legs and hiking boots."
Gayl Waugh

"I have read so many self help books I'm in danger of becoming perfect."
Elaine Rockwell

"My wife shops at Wal-Mart so much that they made her employee of the month. The next month they made her an honorary greeter."
Tyler Carlson

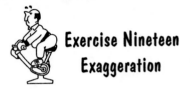

Exercise Nineteen
Exaggeration

This space has been provided for you to work on writing an exaggeration about one of your joke ideas, or premises from the previous chapters.

1.	
2.	
3.	
4.	
5.	
6.	
7.	
8.	
9.	
10.	
11.	
12.	
13.	
14.	
15.	

These formulas should help you punch up your punch lines. Keep in mind several formulas may exist in the same joke. A good punch line doesn't limit itself to just one style. You can have a reverse that is an exaggeration, a combination that has a word play, and so on. Having a good handle on the formulas will make joke writing easier.

Exercise Twenty
Watch A Pro

Watch a professional comedian on television. Take a moment and write down a few jokes that made you laugh. Examine these jokes. Determine the formula that each joke uses. Keep in mind, a good joke may contain several formulas.

JOKES	WORDACE FORMULA
1.	
2.	
3.	
4.	
5.	
6.	
7.	
8.	
9.	
10.	
11.	
12.	
13.	
14.	
15.	

CHAPTER TEN
Joke Structure

Okay, so we have our funny idea turned into a punch line. What next? We must give it structure. For our purposes, I have identified four structures that a joke can take.

<u>Joke Structures</u>

One-Liner, or Set Up/Punch

List Jokes

Anecdotes and Stories

Sight Gags

There are many other structures. Limericks and knock-knock jokes spring to mind. These are the four that are most prevalent in stand-up comedy and public speaking. Be careful not to confuse structure with formula. Simply put, the formula is the gift, the structure is the box that it comes in. Let's break them down one by one.

The most common structure of a joke is the one-liner. This is also called the set-up/punch structure. It consists of two parts. First, the set-up, or information that explains what the joke is about. The second part is the punch line, or the part that gets the laughs. (Most of the **WORDACE** examples were one-liners.)

There are several things to remember about the one-liner.

1. Make sure your set-up and punch line are in the right order.

This may sound a bit silly, but you would be surprised how many beginning comedians make this mistake.

2. Don't give the audience too much information.

Giving away too much information is called "telegraphing" your punch line. Try to give only enough information in your set up to explain the punch line.

3. Eliminate excess verbiage.

There's a simple comedy rule that must be heeded. **The longer your set up, the funnier your punch line has to be.** Include only the information relevant to the joke.

The list style joke is another good structure your jokes can take. Simply put, the subject of the list is stated (your premise) and the punch lines follow in rapid succession. The most common examples of this are David Letterman's "Top 10 List" and Jeff Foxworthy's "You might be a redneck if..."

For Example:

> **You might be a redneck if...**
> ...you go to a family reunion to pick up women.
> ...your family tree does not fork.
> ...when a sign that says "Say No to Crack" reminds you to pull up your jeans.
> ...you've ever been too drunk to fish.
> ...your front porch collapses and kills more than three dogs.

The list is a great structure for getting punch lines out quickly. It is also a marvelous structure for trying to fit a lot of random ideas under one heading. You can use as many punch lines in a list style joke as you want. Any more than ten gets to be too long. A good number to shoot for is five or six.

Anecdotes/Stories

Another structure that is very common in stand-up, and even more so in public speaking, is the humorous anecdote or story. An anecdote is a tall tale told as a small story with a humorous climax.

For Example:

> A minister comes home to his apartment early and finds his wife in bed and the room filled with cigar smoke. He looks down from his tenth-story window and sees a man smoking a big cigar just leaving the building. Enraged, he picks up his refrigerator and throws it out the window, killing the man instantly.
>
> "Why did you do that?" someone yelled from the street. "You killed my priest."
>
> The minister was so distraught that he threw himself out of the window.
>
> A few moments later, three men -- a priest, a minister, and a rabbi-- approach heaven's gate and an angel asks each how he died. "I don't know," says the priest, "except suddenly a refrigerator smashed me into the ground." The minister says, "I threw it. But I was so filled with remorse, I jumped out of the window and killed myself."
>
> "What about you, rabbi?" asks the angel.
>
> "You got me. All I know was I was minding my own business sitting in a refrigerator..."
>
> (Crusty Old Joke)

There are several rules when writing humorous anecdotes.

1. It doesn't have to be true, just funny.

I had a student who wrote a hilarious story about her trip to Amsterdam. The on[e] trouble was that it was ten minutes long, because she told every little detail of the tri[p] Many details were funny. Many were not. I told her to get rid of everything that didn't g[et] a laugh. She said, "But that's not how it really happened." I replied,"I don't care." T[he] chain of events didn't have to be true, just funny.

2. Be physical.

If your story calls for an action, then act it out. If a character is walking up steps, th[en] the comedian should physically walk up those steps. The more vivid you can make yo[ur] story the funnier it will become.

3. Vary the voices.

If your story has a conversation, then vary the voices so the listener always knows ju[st] who is talking. If you can't vary the voices, at least find a way to differentiate t[he] speakers. This can be done with props or even a change in the way that you stand.

Don't talk like this...

...when you can talk like this!

4. Eliminate excess words.

As mentioned before, get rid of everything that doesn't pertain directly to your story. Include only information vital to setting up something funny.

5. Use funny words.

You must find a funny way to say things. Choose your words carefully. This is so important, I will spend more time explaining it later in the book.

6. Have a big finish.

Make sure that your story finishes with a big punch, otherwise the listener will feel cheated. Nothing is more annoying than listening to a long story only to have the ending leave you flat.

Excess Words ⟶

Excess Hair ⟶

Sight Gags

The final structure is called a sight gag. This includes anything visual that the audience can see such as props, or physical comedy, like prat falls. Good examples of sight gags are Steve Martin's arrow through the head or Howie Mandel blowing up a surgical glove with his nose. There are really no hard, fast rules on sight gags. A good sight gag relies on the element of surprise. The good prop comics take an object and use it in a unique and unusual way.

Exercise Twenty-one
Sight Gags

Find five objects in the room you are in. Come up with two humorous uses for each item other than what they are typically used for.

OBJECT	USE
1.	1.
	2.
2.	1.
	2.
3.	1.
	2.
4.	1.
	2.
5.	1.
	2.

CHAPTER ELEVEN
TROUBLE

If your joke doesn't get a laugh, then you've got **TROUBLE**. There could be a simple way to fix it. I have isolated seven possible problems that your joke may have. Use this tool to analyze why your joke didn't work.

Target

Realism

Obscure

Understanding

Blue

Long

Expected punch line

T is for **Target**

Every joke must have a target. The target can be almost anything; person, place, thing, or idea. Keep in mind that some targets are better than others.

The safest target is yourself. Self-depreciating humor is an effective tool used by all humorists and public speakers. Many comedians have made a career of making fun of nothing but themselves.

Self-depreciating humor is particularly effective when used by people in positions of power.

When choosing a target, make your target big. Poke fun at authority, the government, or a celebrity. Don't pick on the "little guy". Pick on someone or something who is not universally loved. When George Bush was president, you could make fun of him all day. A joke targeted at Barbara Bush would rarely get a laugh. The joke may have been a good one, but the target chosen was bad. A good joke begins with an appropriate target.

R is for **Realism**

For an audience member to laugh at a joke, there must be some semblance of reality. A joke must include some portion of truth.

While exaggeration is an important element in humor, it can not be taken too far. Think of the realism of a joke as a rubber band. It can be stretched and stretched, but if it goes too far, it will break. Your joke must contain a sufficient amount of realism in order for it to work.

O is for **Obscure**

The comedian and the audience must have a common point of view. If a comedian jokes about things that the audience doesn't comprehend, then the comedian is making an obscure reference. This is a difficult problem that all humorists must face. A joke about a movie might be a good one, but if the majority of the audience hasn't seen it, then they won't laugh.

Many comedians rely on ethnic; racial, and religious references. If the topic of a joke steps outside the experience of the audience, the joke fails to get a laugh. When crafting your joke make sure the subject and punch line are suited to your target audience.

U is for **Understanding**

Many times a comedian will deliver a joke and for some reason, it will not be heard. There are several possible explanations for this. The comedian can be speaking too softly, the microphone could cut out, or a waitress could drop a tray of drinks just as the punch line is delivered. The audience will not laugh if they can't understand what you are saying. Speak clearly and slowly. Be alert to any technical difficulties which could impair your delivery of the joke.

B is for **Blue**

The term "blue" refers to a joke that is vulgar or offensive. Certain four letter words may turn audience members off. It is my feeling that swear words are a crutch, used when a joke can not stand on its own. A comedian who works too blue has more difficulty making a connection with his audience. On the flip side, I have seen many instances where blue humor and blue language have been used effectively. It takes an experienced comedian to know when it can be used appropriately. I recommend that beginning comedians steer away from the blue language and blue subjects.

L is for **Long**

To quote The Bard, " Brevity is the soul of wit." The longer your set up , the funnier your punch line has to be. If the set up for a joke is too long, the punch line may not be strong enough to support it. The audience then feels like you have wasted their time. Eliminate the excess verbiage from your set ups. Keep only the information that directly pertains to the joke.

E is for **Expected Punch Line**

Surprise is the most important element in comedy. If the audience can see where the joke is headed, the laugh will be lessened, or completely destroyed. It is your job to disguise the punch line until the last possible moment. If the audience has heard the joke before, it will be harder to get a laugh. Good comedy is not like a good movie. If you hear the same joke again, the surprise will be gone. Always try to write fresh material.

<u>The Bottom Line</u>

Sometimes a joke will not work and you can't find anything technically wrong with it. That just means that the joke isn't funny. Don't despair, just write another one!

CHAPTER TWELVE
Random Thoughts On Joke Writing

This chapter is devoted to some random thoughts on joke writing, based on my experience performing and teaching stand-up comedy.

First of all, don't get discouraged. As a joke writer, you must play the percentages. Not every joke you write is going to be a gem. Baseball player Pete Rose has the most hits in the history of baseball (4256). He also holds the record for the most at bats (14053). This is not a coincidence. Keep this in mind as you craft humor. If you keep going to the plate (note pad), you are bound to hit a home run sooner or later. If you write one funny joke for every ten that you write, you are doing well. As you develop your humor muscle, you will find that your success to failure ratio will keep improving. Don't panic. Play the percentages.

Rule of Three

It has been said that the best comedy is written in threes. No one knows why this is -- it just works. The perfect joke has a set up and a punch line, followed by two additional punch lines, or tags.   In essence, you are getting three laughs out of one idea. Jerry Seinfeld is the master at this.

For example:

> I thought the reason I got glasses as a kid was because I
> couldn't tell what my parents looked like. Because every time
> I'd ask my mother to buy me something she would say "what
> do I look like, a bank?"
>
> Because when you're a kid, your parents are the bank. It is
> the only place that you can get money when you're ten. You
> can't walk into Chase Manhattan. The teller is just going to
> say to you, "What do I look like, your mother?"
>
> "Hit the road four eyes!"
>
> (Jerry Seinfeld)

A good comedian also uses the rule of three to set up the tension in a joke. In the next example, two serious secrets to staying young are presented in order to build up the tension for the last secret, the punch line:

> The secret to staying young is to live honestly, eat slowly, and
> lie about your age.
>
> (Lucille Ball)

Most comedians agree that four is too many and two is not enough. Remember the rule of three.

Funny Words

As a comedian, you must find a funny way to say things. One way to accomplish this is to use words in your jokes that sound funny or create a funny image.

In his play, The Sunshine Boys, Neil Simon wrote:

"Words with K in them are funny. Cupcake is funny, tomato is not funny. Cookie is funny. Cucumber is funny. Car key is funny. Cleveland...Cleveland is funny. Maryland is not funny. Then there's chicken. Chicken is funny. Pickle is funny."

Most professional comedians would agree that 'K' sounds are funny. No one knows really why that is.

Try stringing together funny words and phrases in your joke writing. Use funny sounding words rather than bland or common ones.

For example:
        Instead of saying "blender", say "Cuisinart."
        Instead of saying "hotdog", try "frankfurter".
        Kumquat is a funnier sounding fruit than an apple.

Search for funny words with a possible double meaning.

Twinkie	Salami
Meatball	Cupcake

Certain brand name products are inherently funny.

Exlax	Winnebago
Whopper	Preparation H
Alka Seltzer	Ben Gay

Using **alliteration** is also a good technique. Alliteration is a series of words beginning with the same sound.

For example, in describing equestrian show jumping, a comedian said:

"I hate watching **Black Beauty picking plywood** out of her teeth."

You have a great example of alliteration in both the "B" and the "P" sounds.

Finally, you must describe things in a unique and humorous way. Paula Baudeaux, a Comedy College Graduate, described growing old like this:

"The maturing process doesn't bother me, it's the shriveling process I don't care for. You know what I mean? The dried fig effect. The sharpei syndrome. The slow moving glacier of rolled and pleated cheeks, gaining momentum until the whole body collapses into a smoking pile of epidermal sludge."

Gavin turns 80

Isn't this a funnier way of saying, "Gee, I hate getting old"?

Using funny words and stringing together funny phrases is a must for any humorist. Choose your words carefully. Funny words or phrases add spice and color to your jokes.

Exercise Twenty-two
Stupid Stuff List

Remember back in Exercise One when I had you create a "stupid stuff list" in order to laugh at yourself? Pull out that list. (If you have lost it or blew off the assignment, please complete it now!)

From that list, pick one item that is particularly funny.

Create a joke from this item.

The set-up could be :

> You'll never believe what I just did....

> This is embarrassing, I just......

> Has this ever happened to you...

Exercise Twenty-three
Laugh With Others Exercise

Remember back in the Exercise 2 when I had you create a "laugh with others" list? Pull out that list. (If you have lost it or blew off the assignment, please complete it now.)

From that list, pick one item that is particularly funny.

Create a joke from this item.

The set up could be:

>> You'll never believe this...

>> My friend is so dumb...

>> Has this ever happened to you...

Premise	Brainstorm

Exercise Twenty-four
Premise List

Back in Appendix B there is a premise list. Choose a premise from the many on this list that appeals to you.

Create a joke using that premise.

Premise	Brainstorm

CHAPTER THIRTEEN
Delivery

As I have traveled across this country doing comedy, I have noticed a peculiar phenomenon. Most comedians I have met are either great writers or great performers. It is very rare when a comedian can do both well. A good performer with great delivery can get a lot a mileage out of weaker jokes. It may not be what you say, but how you say it, that gets the laughs. This chapter focuses on the six elements of good joke delivery.

Six Elements of Good Delivery:

1. **Confidence**
2. **Memorization**
3. **Vocal Quality**
4. **Body Language**
5. **Eye Contact**
6. **Timing**

1. Confidence. There is an old comedy adage that was made popular in a deodorant commercial. "Never let them see you sweat." This holds true when telling jokes. You must exude total confidence and control, even in the face of impending doom. My favorite adage is "Nero fiddled while Rome burned." You must believe that your material is good even if it may not be. Your confidence will relax the audience. A word of caution: Avoid appearing over confident or cocky. Nothing will turn off an audience faster.

2. Memorization. The whole process of delivery begins here. You must have your material down cold. Nothing causes more damage to a joke than forgetting a punch line. There are no shortcuts. **You must memorize your material.** Know every word, every phrase, every inflection. In the heat of battle your memory will be the first thing to go. If you know your material you will avoid big trouble.

3. Vocal Quality. I have seen many a good joke ruined because the audience couldn't hear it, or because it was delivered too rapidly. The rule to remember is this:

SPEAK UP, SLOW DOWN

Many comedians have a tendency to rush their delivery. This happens because of adrenaline or inexperience. A professional relaxes and takes his time with a joke. Practice telling your joke very slowly. When nervousness hits, your delivery will not be altered too significantly. As a comedian, you are at the mercy of the microphone. Always check the mic for proper volume and sound level before your performance. This allows you to adjust your vocal dynamics accordingly.

4. Body Language and Facial Expressions. Body language and facial expressions are also important elements of good delivery. Proper use of gestures can be really effective during your act. Always avoid negative body language.

For example:

> **Putting a hand in your pocket**
> **Crossing your arms**
> **Slouching**
> **Holding on to the mic stand**

These gestures convey a lack of confidence and are distracting. Try to incorporate positive body language. Stand up straight and face your audience.

Facial expressions are, by far, one of the most important elements in delivery. In communicating your message remember:

> **55% of your message is Visual (facial expression, body**
> **language, everything about your appearance)**
> **38% of your message is Vocal (tone of voice)**
> **7% is Verbal (the actual words you say)**

Good comedians and public speakers need to be aware of this. I have seen comedians bring the house down with just a look. **Practice your facial expressions in the mirror and leave nothing to chance.**

5. Eye Contact. Every good comedian or speaker knows that in order to be effective, he must make eye contact with everyone in the room. Establishing eye contact does two things. First of all, it will draw the audience in and make them a part of your act or presentation. If they are a part of it, they are listening. Establishing eye contact facilitates the listening process. In a stand-up comedy setting, it is harder to establish eye contact with everyone. Bright lights may make it difficult to see anyone. Remember, even if you can't see them, they can see you. Make an effort to scan the room often and make eye contact with all of your audience as you perform.

6. Timing. You might have figured it out by now. I saved the best for last! The most important element of delivery is timing. You have heard it a million times. "He has great timing." Timing is difficult to define.

Jack Benny said it best:

> **"Timing is not so much knowing when to speak, but knowing when to pause."**

Many people think that timing is something that can't be taught. In his book, "Make 'em Laugh, Life Studies of Comedy Writers," Dr. William Fry, Jr. quotes Herbie Baker on timing:

> **"There are no rules. Timing comes from experience. You get a feeling when timing is right."**

For the most part, I agree. Practice will improve your timing. It may take years, it may take days.

There are some important things to remember. Way back in Chapter One we defined laughter as "the emotional release of humorous tension." You must create humorous tension before you can release it. The most common technique is to pause just before a punch line. The pause creates tension, which is relieved by the punch line. Pausing also provides a subtle clue to the audience that a punch line is coming.

Good timing includes knowing when to tell the next joke. I have identified a phenomenon that I will call **The Wave**.

If a comedian is doing well, the laughter comes in waves. A joke is told, the laughter rises, peaks, and begins to come down. A good comedian begins his next joke before the laughter dies all the way down. A diagram will show this better.

THE WAVE

It is important not to "step on" laughs . If a comedian starts talking again too soon, while the laughter is at its height, two things can happen:

1. The audience will not be able to hear over the laughter and will miss the next joke

2. The audience will stop laughing to try to listen to what the comedian is saying.

Either way, it destroys any wave of laughter the comedian is trying to create.

When it comes to timing, there is no substitute for experience. The more you perform, the better your timing will be. The single best piece of advice I can give a new comedian is **perform your act at every opportunity.**

CHAPTER FOURTEEN
Random Thoughts On Delivery

This chapter is devoted to some random thoughts on joke delivery. First of all, the most important thing I can say about delivery is this:

Since the punch line is the most important part of the joke, it only makes sense to pay a little extra attention to it. A good comedian delivers the punch line crisply and clearly, giving it every chance to succeed.

Another good rule on delivery is to keep it conversational. A good speech or comedy routine should be delivered as if there is only one other person in the room. So many inexperienced speakers and comedians are too presentational with their material. This sounds too contrived and stiff, and will turn the audience off. **Keep it loose, relaxed, and conversational.**

Don't Announce
or
Apologize

Deliver the joke, period. So many times you will hear somebody preface a joke by saying, "Here is something really funny." By saying this, you make it twice as difficult. People resist humor if they think you are trying to be funny. Just deliver the joke. The audience will decide whether or not it's funny.

Along these same lines: never apologize for a joke. Often, a comedian will say, "This joke might really bomb..." and often, it does. If you think a joke isn't funny, then don't tell it. By apologizing in advance for a joke, you label yourself a failure.

One of the oldest jokes in the book is:

"How do you get to Carnegie Hall? Practice, practice, practice..."

How do you get good at delivering jokes? Practice, practice, practice!

There is no short cut. You must work at it. Practice your jokes in front of a mirror. Practice your jokes into a tape recorder. Practice on friends and family. Take advantage of every opportunity to practice in front of a live audience. If something isn't quite right, change it, rewrite it, and practice some more. Sooner or later you will get better.

I suggest that new comedians tape record or videotape their shows. Listen to every joke. Analyze what worked and what didn't. This will help you improve your act.

A common question I hear from of my students is, "How do I memorize all my material?" For some, memorization is easy. For some, it is down right impossible. For those people who find memorization difficult, I have but one word for you...

CHEAT!

Before you go on stage, write the key words of your act on a napkin. Take a drink and the napkin with you on stage. Set them on a table or stool. During your act, if you get stuck, go have a nice drink! A quick glance at the napkin will put you back on track. No one will have any idea what you are doing. (Except for those who also own a copy of this book.)

Writing on your hand is a problem if you sweat a lot.

CHAPTER FIFTEEN
Tricks Of The Trade

The little things. This is what separates the good from the great. This chapter focuses on the little tricks that great comedians use to make themselves funnier.

A great comedian knows how to structure his act. When putting together a routine, there are three things to remember.

1. The first 30 seconds are the most important of your show. In the first 30 seconds the audience decides whether or not they like you. Make a good first impression and your job is much easier. I like to view the audience as passengers on a bus. Every time a comedian or speaker takes the stage, the bus is out of control. If you can get a laugh quickly, it puts the audience at ease. It lets them know that somebody competent is driving the bus.

Get a laugh as quickly as you can. Usually a quick joke about yourself or your appearance works best. Then try to get in as many punch lines as you can. Remember the old saying, **"You never have a second chance to make a first impression."**

2. Structure the body of your act correctly. Put the quick hitting material early. These are the jokes that have short set ups and many punch lines. Save the slower, longer set up stuff for later in your show. The theory behind this is that **once you have the audience with you, you can take them where ever you want to go.**

3. We have all heard the phrase, "Leave them wanting more." This could not be more true than when talking about comedy. Save your very best joke for last. The joke that gets the biggest laugh is called your "closer". It is the joke you use to get you off stage. Nothing looks more awkward than when someone gets a good laugh and then tries to follow it up with lesser material. **Save the best for last and leave them laughing.**

SEGUES

A segue is simply what gets you from joke A to joke B. I have identified three major types of segues that comedians use.

1. **The Logical Segue.** The logical segue is one in which one joke logically leads into another. You have all heard this: "Speaking of_____..." This is commonly used to get into your next joke, provided it has something to do with what you were just talking about.

Sometimes you don't have the luxury of having one joke lead into another. Use one of the next two segues in this case.

2. **The Ridiculous Segue.** This is the opposite of the logical segue. This is usually something outlandish or unusual. I have seen many different examples of this.

For example:

> This was about three days ago... No, I'm lying to you. It never happened!
> (Bob Saget)

> About four years ago...no, it was yesterday.
> (Steven Wright)

3. **The Pause.** Many times segues are not used at all. The easiest and most common way to get from joke A to joke B is a simple pause. A comedian pauses a good 2-3 seconds to let the audience know that he is moving on to another thought.

CALLBACKS

A wonderful trick that comedians use is to refer back to an earlier joke or phrase that got a laugh. If this "callback" is used cleverly, it can be an effective running gag throughout the show.

A comedian friend of mine does a joke early in his show about the silly music you hear in adult movies right before people become intimate. He does an impression of the music and he gets a big laugh. Then, throughout the rest of his show, whenever the joke has a sexual theme, he calls back to his earlier joke by doing the impression again. The audience laughs because they feel in on the joke.

In my act, I use a unique phrase as the punch line to an early joke. That phrase keeps popping up all throughout my show as a tag line to various other punch lines.

In my opinion, no other single trick shows that the comedian knows what he is doing as well as the callback. Search your act for places to use callbacks.

SAVERS

A saver is a line or a look that a comedian uses when a joke doesn't work. It is an attempt to "save face" and salvage your dignity by (hopefully) getting a laugh. The saver releases the tension that the audience feels as a result of a joke that didn't work. Johnny Carson was the master of this. In many instances, he was funnier when his jokes were not working.

Example:

That was a new joke...I won't let that get old.

They can't all be gems, folks!

Savers can act as a safety net that keeps you from completely falling flat on your face. Even the very best comedians need and use them.

AD-LIBS

Ad-libs are "spontaneous" quips that comedians utter when unplanned events occur. If you perform or speak, sooner or later something will happen to upset an audience (people dropping things, lighting failures, sound system problems, hecklers...). A good comedian doesn't panic. He treats the interruption like a set-up and provides a quip to keep the audience with him and relieve the tension. In these situations, getting a laugh is easier because almost any line will do. Trust your judgment and let a joke fly.

The term ad-lib is really a misnomer. Many of the great comedians prepare to be spontaneous. In an ad-lib situation, the comedian searches his memory for something he might have heard or used in the past. When he delivers the line and it appears to be spontaneous, although he may have delivered the same line before in a similar situation.

Example :
Comedian: "So, where you from?"
Patron: "Alabama." (or South Dakota, West Virginia, etc.)
Comedian: "I'll talk slower for you then."

Another example would be if there is a loud distraction in the showroom, such as a waitress dropping a tray of drinks, a comedian may respond:

"You can just set that anywhere."

"There will be an opening for a waitress tomorrow."

KNOW YOUR AUDIENCE

A good humorist always tries to learn as much as he can about his audience in advance. Before you perform ask some questions.

1. **Who are they?**
2. **Where are they from?**
3. **Is there a common thread that binds them together?**
4. **Are there any inside jokes or phrases you can use?**

The same material that was appropriate for a late night comedy club audience may not be suitable for the Women's Auxiliary Luncheon. A good comedian will analyze the audience and use the information to his advantage. This technique is called Localizing. Localizing means tailoring your material to fit your specific audience .

One way to localize is to insert into your joke the name of a local person, place, or thing your audience will recognize. In my show, I do a joke about a mall. (How original.) When I'm in another city, I find out the name of a local mall (East Hills Mall). In my joke, the action doesn't just happen at a mall, it happens at the East Hills Mall. ("I was at the East Hills Mall the other day...")

Localizing your material can help you bond with the audience quickly. You are no longer an outsider, you are now one of them. You both have similar points of reference. Knowing something about your audience in advance can make your job as a humorist much easier. It provides sources of material that they will relate to immediately.

HECKLERS

Every now and again, a comedian will have to deal with a heckler.

> **A Heckler is:**
> **An audience member who**
> **disrupts the flow of your show.**

If a heckler shouts out something, stay cool. The first rule in handling the heckler is to let him hang himself. You must get the audience on your side first. If the audience feels the heckler is really annoying, you can respond with almost anything. If, however, the heckler isn't really negative, and you respond with an angry put down, the audience may turn on you. They may feel your response is inappropriate and stop liking you. You must match your response with the type of heckler that you are facing.

In my travels, I have identified three major types of hecklers:

> **1. The Joiner**
> **2. The Helper**
> **3. The Idiot**

1. The Joiner is an audience member who gets caught up in the emotion of the moment. Rarely do they shout out anything negative. The joiner just wants to participate in the show. Be gentle with the joiner.

2. The Helper is a heckler who thinks they are doing you a favor. They usually shout out things at inappropriate times just to see how you will react. The helper may be negative or just mildly irritating. Be firm but polite with the helper.

3. The Idiot is a heckler who shouts out negative insults or babbles incoherently. This worst of all types of hecklers is often drunk, which means he can be nasty. When dealing with an idiot, go for the throat.

Most comedians have developed stock lines to combat the hecklers' interruptions.

For example:

"I don't come down to Burger King and knock the broom out of your hand when you're working."

"When I wrote my show I don't remember you having a speaking part."

It is not a bad idea to have a few insults memorized. Almost any joke book will give you some ideas. Memorize enough insults to fit all three types of hecklers. As you become more experienced and better able to read an audience you will be able to use your ad-lib skills in these situations.

Another rule, when handling hecklers, is **never let them have the last word.** You must always remain in control while you are on stage. The beautiful thing is that you have a microphone. You will always be louder. Use that to your advantage.

Keep in mind that the heckler only exists if you notice he exists. Sometimes the best course of action is to ignore the heckler entirely.

Public speakers rarely have hecklers. What they do have is annoying interruptions or distractions. A wise speaker will have a humorous remark prepared for any possible situation.

CHAPTER SIXTEEN
Frequently Asked Questions

Here are some questions commonly asked by my Comedy College students:

1. My friends tell me I'm funny. Should I pursue a career in comedy?

Being funny with your friends, or being a cut-up around the water cooler has very little to do with being funny on stage. Some of the funniest comedians I know are not particularly funny off stage. The ability to be funny in a show setting is a different animal completely. It is good that your friends think you are funny, but don't expect it to be an easy transition. About all I can say is that you have more of a chance than someone whose friends think he is a total bore.

2. How do I overcome stage fright?

This is a common problem for beginners. It can be terrifying at first. The old adage of picturing the audience in their underwear is silly. I say, if you can picture yourself on stage in only your underwear, and you still feel comfortable, then you have stage fright licked. Another thing I like to point out is that you are not doing brain surgery. If you screw up and nobody laughs, big deal! Stand-up comedy is not a life and death matter. Don't get me wrong, comedy is big business and should be taken seriously. But if you bomb occasionally, life does go on. **Don't be afraid to fail.** It is the only way you learn.

3. Is it okay to do someone else's material?

NO, NO, a thousand times NO! This makes you a hack and a thief. Thieves are frowned upon in the business. Jokes are how a comedian makes a living. If you steal one, it is similar to stealing tools from a carpenter. You are robbing a man of his livelihood. You must write and perform your own material. Resist the temptation to steal from another comedian. If another comic does a line that you like, the proper thing is to offer to buy it from him. Writing your own material will save you a lot of headaches (and possible lawsuits) in the long run.

4. What is the best advice you can give a beginning humorist?

A beginning humorist needs three things to get ahead. They are: stage time, stage time, and more stage time. **When you are starting out you must perform every chance you get.** The more you do it, the better you get. You have to be creative sometimes. Search every situation for an opportunity to perform.

5. Do I need a promotional kit? What goes in one?

If you want to work professionally, you must have a promo kit. A promo kit is your calling card to the world. **A basic promo kit consists of a head shot and a bio.** Your head shot is a black & white 8 x 10 photograph of you. It can be serious or silly but it must be eye-catching. Have your name printed at the bottom. You also need a biography, or bio. This is one sheet of paper that tells a little about you and some of the places you have worked. When you are starting out, you won't have much to put on a bio. You must be creative to fill the page. It is okay to embellish the truth, but **never lie on your bio.**

6. Do I need a video tape?

Many places will ask to see a video tape of your work. **This tape should be about 15 minutes of your best material.** It needs to be an unedited, live show. The sound and lighting need to be good, as well. A good crowd response is just as important as the content of your performance.

7. How much performance material do I need to begin working?

The first goal you should set for yourself is **15 minutes.** If you have 15 minutes of humorous material then you can start looking for work. **Your ultimate goal is to have one hour of proven material.** Work toward this goal in fifteen minute increments. The more time you have, the better gigs you can land. Keep in mind, however, **the amount of material must be of quality.**

8. I have enough funny material. How do I get work?

There are countless ways a comedian can get work. I believe the most effective way is networking. In this business, the old adage is true: "It's not <u>what</u> you know, it's <u>who</u> you know." There are also a multitude of agents whose sole purpose is to find comedians.

9. But can I make a living?

At the highest levels, comedy can pay huge bucks. Humorists are always in demand. Even at the middle levels, a talented comedian or speaker can make a good living. Starting out, however, things are a bit different. In order to learn your craft and build your reputation, sometimes it is necessary to work for next to nothing. **Always try to get some form of compensation, be it a free meal, free drinks, or a letter of recommendation.**

10. What is best advice anybody ever gave you?

First, do your time. **If you are supposed to do 15 minutes, do 15 minutes.** Don't do 14 minutes. Don't do 16 minutes. Don't be a mic hog. Second, play nice with others. When you are starting out, there is no reason to have an attitude. You are not that funny!

ALRIGHT BUB... TIME'S UP!

CONCLUSION

Well, there it is, everything you ever wanted to know about comedy. Let me stress that, while I believe that this is the most comprehensive and user friendly book on comedy out there, it is by no means the final word. Comedy is a subjective thing, it is not an exact science. For every idea, rule, or thought on comedy, there is an exception.

The ideas, thoughts, and theories expressed in this book have been used to teach comedy for many years with an astounding record of success. People from all walks of life have attended and been successful using the techniques presented in this book. There are many schools of thought regarding comedy. But few schools have had the success rate that Gavin Jerome's Comedy College has enjoyed. If you read and follow the ideas in this book, you will improve your sense of humor and learn to write and deliver jokes. You will also have a better understanding of some of the little tricks that comedians use.

This much information can be overwhelming at first. Relax, this is supposed to be fun. Do the exercises, work and practice hard. You will get funnier. Trust me!

Insert your head here

Good night folks...
You've been great!

GLOSSARY

Alliteration: A series of words beginning with the same sound.

Analogy: A comparison between two things that appear dissimilar.

Anecdote: A tall tale told as a small story with a humorous climax.

Blue: A comedy term meaning that a joke or act is too dirty, often using swear words or vulgar premises.

Bomb: Doing poorly. Not receiving many laughs at all.

Brainstorming: The creative process of generating a large number of ideas.

Broadcast Media: Anything that can be viewed or that is presented to the viewer.

Callback: Creating a running gag by calling back to a previously mentioned punch line or phrase.

Closer: The final joke at the end of your show.

Combination: Takes the characteristics from two different items and blends them in a funny way.

Comedy: Making a connection with the audience that produces laughter.

Definition: Defining a word in a comical way.

Edit: The process of separating the best ideas from ones that are not as strong.

Exaggeration: A quality of something is stretched to the point of absurdity.

Feature act: Goes on second. Usually performs 30-35 minutes.

Hack: A comedian who uses stock or stolen jokes.

Headliner: The main performer. Usually the last performer. Does 45 minutes to an hour show.

Heckler: An audience member who disrupts the flow of your show.

Hell-gig: A situation not conducive to comedy. A loud, rowdy night club where it is difficult to do your act. Or anywhere you can hear the bowling ball hitting the pins.

IBET: Acronym for the four steps to joke writing.

Idea: The basic starting point of a joke (ie. what the joke is about).

Kill: Doing exceptionally well. Getting a huge amount of laughs.

Laughter: The emotional release of humorous tension.

List Jokes: A structure in which the subject of the list (premise) is stated and punch lines follow in rapid succession.

Localizing: Tailoring your material to fit a specific audience.

M.C.: Master of Ceremonies. Goes on first and usually introduces the other acts.

Observation: An observation draws relationships that we wouldn't normally see, based on a premise that we perceive to be true.

One-liner: A joke structure consisting of a set-up and a punch line.

Opener: Your first joke.

Personal Experiences: A source of comedy. Anything having to do with you or things that have happened to you or someone you know.

Physical Comedy: Anything that produces laughs using the performer's body. This includes prat falls, making faces, etc.

Premise: See Idea.

Print Media: A source of humor. Anything on a printed page.

Punchline: The pay off. The part of the joke that gets the laugh.

Reverse: An unexpected switch in point of view in which you turn around a normal sequence of events.

Savers: A line or look used when a joke doesn't get a laugh.

Segue: What gets you from joke A to joke B.

Sense of Humor: The ability to look at things from a whimsical or offbeat perspective .

Set-Up: The part of the joke that gives the listener information. It "sets up" the listener for the punch line.

Sight Gags: A visual joke, using props and/or physical comedy.

Stock Jokes: Jokes which are widely used by many comedians over the years.

Switching: Transforming inadequate or bad jokes into useable material.

Tag Line: A quick punch line that follows another punch line.

Target: The person, place, thing, or idea at which a joke is directed.

Tie Together: The process in which you take a joke idea and turn it into a finished joke.

Timing: The art of knowing when to speak and when not to speak.

TROUBLE: An acronym for the seven reasons why a joke doesn't work.

WHEXT: Short for "what next".

WHIFF Short for "what if".

Word-Play: The misuse or uncommon use of words or cliches.

WORDACE: Acronym for the seven joke writing formulas.

Appendix A

Exercise Twenty-five
Personal Feeling Exercise

Sometimes the best comedy comes from things that you are passionate about. From the answers to these questions write some jokes. Try to write one joke about each of these seven feelings.

I REALLY HATE:

1.	
2.	
3.	

I REALLY LOVE:

1.	
2.	
3.	

I REALLY GET ANGRY WHEN:

1.	
2.	
3.	

I GET REALLY HAPPY WHEN:

1.	
2.	
3.	

I AM REALLY CONFUSED BY:

1.	
2.	
3.	

I GET REALLY SCARED WHEN:

1.	
2.	
3.	

I AM REALLY AMAZED BY:

1.	
2.	
3.	

Exercise Twenty-six
Noun Exercise

When all else fails I like to brainstorm a list of nouns. If you remember from your grade school days (or Saturday morning cartoons), a noun is a person, place, or thing. Now, from this list, try to write one joke from each of the categories. (i.e. a joke about something from your person list, place list, and thing list.

If done correctly, this exercise should yield 3 different jokes.

PERSON	PLACE	THING

Exercise Twenty-seven
Create Your Own Anecdote / Story

Exercise Twenty-eight
Create Your Own "List" Structure Joke

Appendix B

Here is a list of premises. This is by no means a comprehensive list of all the possible premises a joke can take, but it should get you started. Skim this list and find a topic that interests you. Keep in mind that many times you will have to narrow the focus. For example, if you choose holiday, pick the one that appeals to you.

PREMISE LIST

A.A.
Accidents
Aging
Airports
Animals
Accountants
Adultery

Babies
Bachelors
Baldness
Banks
Barbers
Bars
Beauty parlors
Bosses
Brides
Beverages

Cars
Cabs
Camp
Cheapness
Cheating
Church
Clothes
College
Commercials
Computers
Cooking
Crime

Dreams
Drugs
Drinking
Driving

Eating
Economy
Employment
Engagement
Exercise
Excuses

Fairy tales
Family
Famous sayings
Farmers
Fashion
Fat
Fathers
Fishing
Funeral

Gags
Gambling
Gangsters
Garbage
Gifts
Government
Graduation
Grandparents
Game Shows

History
Holidays
Hometowns
Honesty
Honeymoons
Hospitals
Hotels
Husbands
Hunting

Illness
IRS
Inflation
Insurance
Inventions

Jail
Jobs
Jogging

Kids
Kindergarten
Kissing

Landlords
Lateness
Laziness
Liars
Loneliness
Love
Luck
Lawyers

Dancing
Dating
Death
Dentists
Dieting
Divorce
Doctors

Habits
Hair
Happiness
Health
Heaven
Hillbillies
Hippies

Mail
Manners
Menopause
Marriage
Maternity
Medicine
Memory

Men
Mistakes
Models
Money
Mom
Mother-in-law
Movies
Music
Military

Names
Nature
Neighbors
News
Noise
Noses

Obscenity
Old maids
Opera

Parking
Peace
Pets
Plumbers
Police
Pollution
Pregnancy
Presidents
Prostitution
Proverbs

Questions
Quips
Quotes

Relatives
Real Estate
Reading
Reincarnation
Rejection
Religion
Remedies

Respect
Restaurant

School
Science
Sports
Secretaries
Seasons
Servants
Sex
Shopping
Shortness
Sins
Small towns
Smog
Smoking
Speeding
Stupidity
Success

Tackiness
Talking
Tall
Taxes
Teachers
Telephones
Television
Thin
Time
Toughness
Travel
Trust
Twins

Ugliness
Unemployment
Unions
Used cars

Vacations
Vanity
Vegetarians
Virginity

Voting

Waiters
Weather
Wives
Wills
Women
Work
Worry

X-rays

Youth
Y.M.C.A.

Zebra
Zodiac

Gavin's Appendix

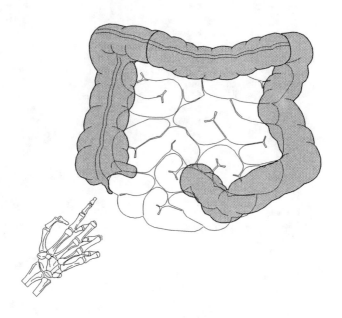

NOTES

The Comedy College How-To Handbook

Where do I go from here? Check out these other great resources to keep your comedic juices flowing!

 Check out Gavin's website for a wealth of resources, links and a library of other funny books! Click on over to www.gavinjerome.com

 Get the Ebook version of the Gavin Jerome Comedy College Home Study Course! Click on over to www.2becomeastandupcomedian.com

 Check out Gavin's other Ebook Home Study Course that helps you become a speaker! www.2becomeaprofessionalspeaker.com

 Check out Gavin Jerome's Professional Motivational Speaking website. Click over to www.moralemechanic.com

1-800-96-GAVIN